PREPARING FOR
First Holy Communion

A GUIDE FOR FAMILIES

ELAINE MAHON

VERITAS

Published 2013 by Veritas Publications
7–8 Lower Abbey Street, Dublin 1, Ireland
publications@veritas.ie
www.veritas.ie

ISBN 978-1-84730-401-8

Illustrations: front cover, p. 7, 16, 18, 19, 20, 21, 25, 27, 32 © Can Stock
Photo Inc./lenm; p. 8 & 11 © Can Stock Photo Inc./jpegwiz; p. 13 © Can
Stock Photo Inc./zzve; p. 16 & 17 © Can Stock Photo Inc./casaltamoiola

For the Walsh family. May it help them and all domestic churches to
share faith together.

10 9 8 7 6 5 4 3 2

A catalogue record for this book is available from the British Library.

Designed by Lir Mac Cárthaigh, Veritas
Printed in Ireland by Walsh Colour Print, Kerry

Veritas books are printed on paper made from the wood pulp of
managed forests. For every tree felled, at least one tree is planted,
thereby renewing natural resources.

1. We are Part of One Family, God's Family

If you are reading this book, it is likely that a child in your family is preparing to celebrate his/her First Holy Communion, or First Eucharist. Congratulations! This is a special and important time for you and your child. It is another step on the journey that you began on the day that you presented him/her for the sacrament of Baptism. It was then that you promised to be your child's 'first and best' teacher in the ways of faith. By helping him/her to prepare for First Holy Communion, you are doing just that.

This book is divided into eight parts, each of which focuses on a different aspect of the Mass. Each part of the book ends with a 'PJ Prayer' to be said before bed. We include this so that children learn that Mass is not the only place where they can pray, or talk to God. Certain Mass responses are highlighted throughout the book, and a full list of prayers for the Mass is given at the end.

It is our hope that this book will help you to understand the celebration of the Mass better yourself, and in doing so to be more confident in explaining it to your child. However, the *best* way to teach children about the Mass is to celebrate it with them, as a family, in the context of your own parish community. Our aim is not just to teach children what happens at Mass, it is to help them to grow in understanding and appreciation for it, so that they will be better able to participate in it.

> **A Prayer for Parents and Families**
> Loving God,
> We thank you for the gift of our faith.
> Thank you for the generations gone before us, who passed on their faith to us.
> Help us to encourage _____ (*your child's name*) in his/her journey of faith, especially during this special time of preparation for First Communion.

We all have a family that we belong to, but every family is different. **Who is in your family?**

Stick a photograph of your family here, or draw a picture.

We are also part of a much bigger family. This family is made up of millions and millions of people spread all over the world. Can you guess what family this is? It's **God's family**! God is like the father or mother of our big family, and we are all God's children – like brothers and sisters of one another.

You became part of God's family on the day you were **baptised**. Find out about this day:

Who was there on the day of your Baptism?

Who chose your name, or names, and why?

Who were chosen to be your godparents?

Why were they chosen as your godparents?

As children of God, and because God loves each one of us, we can always talk to him. **The word we use for talking to God is 'praying'.** We pray to God to thank him for all the things we have, to ask for his help and to ask him to bless other people.

We can pray to God anywhere and at any time. We can use our own words or we can say the prayers we have learned at home and in school, which other people also pray. Praying to God helps us to get to know God better and to feel his great love for us.

PJ Prayer

Loving God,
Thank you for my family.
Help us to take care of one other, and to show our love for one another.
Keep us all safe through the night.
Amen.

2. We Gather Together to Celebrate

At the beginning of his public ministry, one of the first things that Jesus did was to call together a group of men and women who would share in his life and in his work. Chief among these were the twelve Apostles, but there were many other friends (or disciples) who travelled with Jesus, who listened to him, and who believed that he was the Messiah that God had promised. They were the first community of believers.

Today, we gather together in our own place and time as a community of believers, responding to the invitation given by Jesus at the Last Supper to 'Do this in memory' of him. We believe that Jesus is present with us as we join together to celebrate his life, death, resurrection and ascension.

This first section of the book will help your child to understand that Mass is a special time when we gather together to celebrate as members of God's family. It also introduces the priest's greeting, 'The Lord be with you', which may be said up to four times during the celebration of the Mass.

A Prayer for Parents and Families

Loving God,
Thank you for the gift of our community of faith, who gather together in your name each week.
We are mindful of those around the world who cannot come together to celebrate their faith, either because of illness or fear of persecution.
Help us not to take our weekly celebration of the Mass for granted.
Amen.

Think of the times when **your family** gathers together:

For birthdays

At Christmas

For Baptisms

God's family also gathers together. We do this in a special way on Sundays, when we go to the church.

Before Mass begins, take a look around the church. See if you can find the following:

Checklist

- [ ] **Altar:** The priest celebrates Mass on this special table.

- [ ] **Ambo:** The readings are read from this stand.

- [ ] **Tabernacle:** The place where Holy Communion is kept after Mass.

- [ ] **Sanctuary Lamp:** A light which reminds us that the Risen Jesus, the Bread of Life, is present.

- [ ] **Statues:** There is usually a statue of Mary in the church. There may be others too.

- [ ] **Candles:** These are lit during Mass.

- [ ] **Stations of the Cross:** Pictures or sometimes statues showing the story of how Jesus died.

When Mass begins, we stand and sing a song or hymn. **Singing hymns is another way of praying to God**. Next, the priest invites us all to make a special sign – **the Sign of the Cross** – to show that we are there because we are part of God's family and followers of Jesus. Then the priest welcomes us to Mass by saying, '**The Lord be with you**'.

How do we respond?

The Lord be with you

And with your Spirt

PJ Prayer

Loving God,
Thank you for my family at home, my family in school, and my family in the Church.
Help me to pray with all of these families, so that I will become closer to you.
Keep us all safe through the night.
Amen.

3. We Celebrate God's Forgiveness

One of the first things we do when we gather together for Mass is to acknowledge that there have been ways in which we have failed ourselves, each other and God, and we ask for forgiveness for those times. This is called the Penitential Rite. The two prayers most commonly used during the Penitential Rite are the *Confiteor* ('I Confess …') and the *Kyrie* ('Lord, have mercy').

You can help to prepare for the Penitential Rite by encouraging your child to look back over the week and to think about anything he/she did for which he/she is sorry. Remind your child that God is always ready to forgive us, like the loving father in Jesus' parable of the Prodigal Son.

Later in the Mass, during the Our Father, we pray that God will '… forgive us our trespasses as we forgive those who trespass against us'. The two-fold nature of forgiveness is clear here: we ask God to forgive us *as* we forgive others. We cannot ask for forgiveness without being willing to forgive. After the Our Father, we share with one another a gesture of reconciliation and solidarity: a sign of peace.

The Mass is therefore a celebration of God's love for us and of his forgiveness. We, in turn, share this love and forgiveness with others. We help children to understand this in the pages that follow.

A Prayer for Parents and Families

Loving God,
You sent your Son, Jesus, to reveal to us the depth of your love.
His words and actions showed us how to be reconciled with you, with others and with ourselves.
Help us to teach our child about your never-ending love and forgiveness.
Amen.

As **friends of Jesus**, we always do our best to live in the way he asked, by loving God and one another. But sometimes we say or do things that are wrong, or that hurt others. When we realise that we have done something wrong, we need to **say that we are sorry**.

When we gather together at Mass on Sundays, we ask for God's forgiveness.

Can you think of a time when ...

You had mean thoughts about other people?

You did something that you shouldn't have done?

You were supposed to do something but you didn't?

You said something that was hurtful?

We know that **God always loves us** and that he will always forgive us. At Mass, we celebrate this forgiveness. How lucky we are to know **that God will always be there for us**, waiting to show us that he loves us, no matter what!

One of the ways that we thank God for his love is by **sharing it with others**. Because God always forgives us, we must always be ready to forgive other people. We can show that we forgive other people later on in the Mass, when we share a **sign of peace** with each other. This sign of peace shows that we forgive those who have hurt us and that we want to share God's love and forgiveness with all of his people.

What do we say to each other when we share a sign of peace?

PJ Prayer

Confiteor

I confess to almighty God
and to you, my brothers and sisters,
that I have greatly sinned
in my thoughts and in my words,
in what I have done
and in what I have failed to do,
through my fault, through my fault,
through my most grievous fault;
therefore I ask blessed Mary ever-Virgin,
all the Angels and Saints,
and you, my brothers and sisters,
to pray for me to the Lord our God. Amen.

4. We Listen to the Word of God

During the next part of the Mass, we listen to readings from Sacred Scripture. This part of the Mass is called the Liturgy of the Word. We believe that the Bible is God's Word for us; it is God's way of communicating with us.

Usually, the first reading we hear at Mass is taken from the oldest part of Sacred Scripture, the Old Testament. In the Old Testament we learn that God created the world and everything in it and we hear about God's relationship with his people up to the coming of Jesus.

The next Scripture passage we hear at Mass is taken from the Book of Psalms, which is also in the Old Testament. The Psalms are hymns of praise. At Mass, we have a response to the Psalm that everyone says or sings together.

The Second Reading is taken from one of the books of the New Testament that comes after the Gospels. For example, it might be a passage taken from a letter written by St Paul to one of the early Christian communities, or it might be a reading from the Acts of the Apostles, which tells us about the establishment of the early Church.

After the Second Reading, an acclamation (usually 'Alleluia') is sung as a way of welcoming the Gospel reading. In the Gospels, we read about the life and teachings of Jesus, who was sent by God as the greatest sign of his love for us. Jesus showed us how to relate to others and how to relate to God.

The homily and Prayer of the Faithful follow the Gospel. In the homily the priest helps us to understand God's Word and suggests the ways in which it can be put into practice in our own lives. The prayers which follow are the prayers of the community at this time.

In the next set of pages, we want to help children to understand that the readings from the Bible are different from anything else that we read or listen to. They are not stories *about* God, but they are actually God's words *to* us. We need to listen to them with an open heart, and to allow them to become part of our lives.

A Prayer for Parents and Families

Loving God,
Thank you for the gift of your Word, which we hear each week at Mass.
May it help us and our children to grow in love for you and for others.
May we treat it with respect, and listen to it with an open heart and mind.
Amen.

During the next part of the Mass, we listen to **stories from the Bible**. The Bible is a holy and important book because it is God's Word for us. It is one of the ways that God speaks to us today.

In the Bible we hear stories about:

- How God made the world and everything in it
- How God loves all that he created
- How God called people to bring his message to the world
- How God sent Jesus to show the people the best way to live.

The most important stories that we hear at Mass are the **stories about Jesus**. These are written in four books called the Gospels. In the Gospels we hear about:

- How Jesus was born in a stable in Bethlehem
- How he grew up in Nazareth
- How he told people all about God and God's love for them
- How he suffered and died on the cross.

At Mass, **the priest reads a story** from one of the Gospels. We might hear about how Jesus healed someone who was sick, or about when he calmed a storm.

We might listen to a story that Jesus told his friends, like the one about the lost sheep or the good neighbour. Each of the stories we hear teaches us something about God and **how God wants us to live**.

The readings from the Gospels are the most **special and important stories** that we will ever hear. At Mass, we do particular things to show just how special they are:

- We stand up
- We sing 'Alleluia' to welcome the Gospel
- We make the sign of the cross on our forehead, our lips and our heart.

Then we are ready to hear **what message Jesus has for us today**.

What do we say at the end of the Gospel?

The Gospel of the Lord

PJ Prayer

Loving God,
Thank you for the stories in the Bible.
Help me to listen to them carefully,
    so that I can hear your message.
Help me to act on that message, so
    that I can show my love for you
    and for others.
Keep us all safe through the night.
Amen.

5. We Give Thanks

The next part of the Mass is called the Liturgy of the Eucharist. The word Eucharist means 'thanksgiving'. It begins with the Offertory Procession, when we bring gifts of bread and wine to the altar. These gifts, made by the work of human hands, will be transformed into the Body and Blood of Christ. At this time, we also give our monetary gift for the Church, so that it can continue its mission to our parish and diocesan communities.

After the Prayer over the Gifts, the priest begins to pray the Eucharistic Prayer, a long prayer of thanksgiving, during which the people pray or sing the *Sanctus* ('Holy Holy'), the *Mystery of Faith* and the great *Amen*.

As part of the Eucharistic Prayer, we recall what Jesus did at the Last Supper: He took the bread, blessed it, broke it and shared it, saying 'This is my Body' and 'This is my Blood'. He asked us to 'Do this in memory' of him. This part of the Mass (known as the 'consecration') is the moment at which the bread and wine is changed into the Body and Blood of Christ. It still looks like bread and wine but it is now no longer bread and wine.

This is a mystery of our faith and so is something that we can never fully understand ourselves, let alone explain to children. What we want to do, at this stage in their development, is to make children aware that what we receive in Holy Communion is more than just ordinary bread and/or wine.

Before reading the 'Prayer before Holy Communion' as your PJ Prayer this evening, spend some time discussing it with your child. In the beginning, it is a good idea to pray this prayer with children at Mass, rather than just telling them to do so. This will help them to understand how important it is to prepare well to receive Holy Communion.

A Prayer for Parents and Families

Loving God,
We thank you for all that you have given to us, and especially for our children.
Help us to nurture in them a deep sense of gratitude for all that they have.
May we give all glory and honour to you.
Amen.

During the next part of Mass, **we give thanks to God**.
Think of all the things that God has given to you:

A family to love and take care of you

Teachers to help you to learn

Friends to play with

The most precious gift that God gave to the world was **the gift of Jesus**. God sent Jesus into the world to show us how to live and how to love. On the night before Jesus died, he gave us his Body and Blood as our spiritual food, in the form of bread and wine.

While he was at supper with his friends, he took a piece of bread, blessed it, broke it and shared it. He said, '**Take and eat. This is my body**'.

Then, he took a cup of wine, blessed it, and gave it to his Apostles.

He said, '**Take and drink. This is my blood**'.

Then he asked his friends to do this again, after he had gone, **as a way of remembering him**. The next day, Jesus died on the cross.

Three days later, **Jesus rose to new life**, but the Risen Jesus could not stay with his friends forever because he belonged with God the Father in heaven. His friends remembered what Jesus had said, and so they gathered together, took bread and wine, blessed it in the way he had told them and shared it together. They knew that **the Risen Jesus was with them** when they did this.

We too are friends of Jesus and so, at Mass, **we gather together** as he asked us to. In memory of what Jesus did, the priest takes the bread, blesses it and breaks it. We know that when we do this, **the Risen Jesus is with us**.

Fill in the blanks to pray the Mystery of Faith:

We proclaim your _____, O Lord, and profess your

_____

until you come again.

6. We Share Jesus, The Bread of Life

This part of the Mass begins with the Our Father, the prayer Jesus taught his disciples when they asked him how they should pray. Following the Our Father we share a 'sign of peace' with one another. The *Agnus Dei* ('Lamb of God') is then prayed, after which we kneel and prepare to receive Holy Communion.

Children can receive Holy Communion either in their hand or on their tongue. The important thing is that they receive it with reverence. All who are able are asked to fast from food and drink for at least one hour prior to the reception of Holy Communion as a mark of respect for what we are to receive.

In the pages that follow, the 'Prayer after Holy Communion' is introduced. Again, go through this prayer carefully with your child. Some prompts are included to help you to do so. The main thing we want children to understand is that receiving Jesus, the Bread of Life, helps us to live in the way he asked us. It is the food that nourishes our faith.

As with the 'Prayer before Holy Communion', pray the 'Prayer after Holy Communion' with your child to help them establish it as part of their routine.

A Prayer for Parents and Families

Lord Jesus,
We believe that you come to us in Holy Communion,
because you have said it and your Word is true.
May our participation in the Mass help us to live our lives as witnesses to the love you revealed to the world.
Amen.

Think of the **meals** that you and your family share together:

Christmas dinner

Birthday cakes

Family picnics

Holy Communion is the **special meal** that the friends of Jesus share together. While it looks and tastes like bread and wine, it is actually the Risen Jesus that we receive. That is the amazing thing: Jesus promised that he would be with his friends forever and, through Holy Communion, he is!

We get ready to share the Risen Jesus, the Bread of Life, by praying the 'Prayer before Communion' quietly. Holy Communion is not ordinary bread. It is food that helps us to **grow in love with God and for other people**. When we receive Holy Communion and hear the words, 'The Body of Christ', we respond 'Amen' to show we understand this.

After we receive Holy Communion, we return quietly to our seats, and say the 'Prayer after Holy Communion'. Look at each part of the prayer and think about what it means:

Lord Jesus, I love and adore you.
You're a special friend to me.
Welcome, Lord Jesus, O welcome,
Thank you for coming to me.

Thank you, Lord Jesus, O thank you,
For giving yourself to me,
Make me strong to show your love
Wherever I may be.

Be near me, Lord Jesus, I ask you to stay
Close by me for ever and love me, I pray,
Bless all of us children in your loving care,
And bring us to heaven to live with you there.

I'm ready now, Lord Jesus,
To show how much I care,
I'm ready now to give your love
At home and everywhere.
Amen.

We begin by welcoming Jesus. We know that after we receive Holy Communion, Jesus is with us in a very special way.

Next, we say thank you to Jesus for coming to us in Holy Communion and ask for his help to show his love to others.

Then we ask Jesus to bless us and all people. We know that, one day, we will live with Jesus forever in heaven.

Now that we have received Jesus, the Bread of Life, we are able to share his love with others.

Prayer after Communion
Lord Jesus, I love and adore you.
You're a special friend to me.
Welcome, Lord Jesus, O welcome,
Thank you for coming to me.

Thank you, Lord Jesus, O thank you,
For giving yourself to me,
Make me strong to show your love
Wherever I may be.

Be near me, Lord Jesus, I ask you to stay
Close by me for ever and love me, I pray,
Bless all of us children in your loving care,
And bring us to heaven to live with you there.

I'm ready now, Lord Jesus,
To show how much I care,
I'm ready now to give your love
At home and everywhere.

7. We Go in Peace

At the end of the celebration of the Mass we are blessed and sent forth from the church to live what we have heard, and to put into action the message of Jesus in our own place and time.

Saint Teresa of Ávila was a Spanish woman who lived in the sixteenth century. One of her most quoted prayers is entitled 'Christ Has No Body'. This prayer can help us to understand that the work begun by Jesus will only continue if we commit ourselves to carrying it on. Jesus' message was one of radical love, compassion and inclusivity. As his followers, that is our task too.

Christ has no body but yours,
No hands, no feet on earth but yours,
Yours are the eyes with which he looks
Compassion on this world,
Yours are the feet with which he walks to do good,
Yours are the hands, with which he blesses all the world.
Yours are the hands, yours are the feet,
Yours are the eyes, you are his body.
Christ has no body now but yours,
No hands, no feet on earth but yours,
Yours are the eyes with which he looks
compassion on this world.
Christ has no body now on earth but yours.

In the pages that follow, we want children to understand that they can play their part in bringing God's love to the world, in being his hands and feet. Our participation in the Mass strengthens us to do this.

A Prayer for Parents and Families

Lord Jesus,
Your life brought hope to the world.
You taught us that there is another, better way to live.
Give us the grace to follow in your footsteps in the reality of our own lives.
Amen.

At the end of Mass, the priest blesses us and tells us to 'Go in peace, glorifying the Lord by your life'. This means that, after we leave Mass, we should try our best to **live in the way God wants us to**. We have listened to stories from the Bible, and we have received the Bread of Life, so we know that the Risen Jesus is with us, helping us. He wants us to share his love with the world.

Here are some ideas for ways in which you can **share God's love with the world**. Try your best to do these things at all times, but especially after you have been to Mass. Each time you do one of these nice things, colour a panel in the church windows below. See if you can colour them all!

- Help your family to prepare a meal.
- Say sorry to someone you weren't nice to.
- Call to see a neighbour who is living alone.
- Give a hug to someone who takes care of you and say 'thank you' to them.
- Pick up any litter in your school yard or around your house.
- Say a prayer for someone you know who is sick.
- Visit a church and ask for help to light a candle.
- Be polite: say 'please' and 'thank you'.
- Give away one of your best smiles.

How do we respond to the priest at the end of Mass?

Go in peace, glorifying the Lord by your life.

PJ Prayer

Loving God,
Open my ears so that I may hear those who ask me for help.
Open my eyes so that I may see what needs to be done.
Open my heart so that I can love as Jesus did.
Keep us all safe through the night.
Amen

8. We Continue to Live as Friends of Jesus

The journey that your family undertook in preparing for your child's First Holy Communion did not begin when you started to read this book. Neither, then, will it end because you have finished it, or because the First Holy Communion celebration has come and gone. The Eucharist is a mystery, and it takes a lifetime to even begin to understand it.

If you have enjoyed reading this book with your child, and if you have come to understand the Eucharist better because of it, think about how you might continue your child's faith journey over the coming years. It is a sad reality that many children celebrate their First Holy Communion with great enthusiasm and then don't continue to go to Mass until they begin to prepare for the Sacrament of Confirmation.

Consider continuing the practices that have been suggested in this book to help your child to grow in faith over the next few years:

- Say your own 'PJ Prayer' at night
- Read stories from the Bible and chat about them
- Encourage your child to perform acts of charity or 'good deeds' as an expression of their desire to live like Jesus
- Help your child to participate fully and actively in the Mass.

Remember that by joining with your parish community for Mass, you are fulfilling Jesus' final request: 'Do this in memory of me.' In his name, we come together to celebrate.

A Prayer for Parents and Families

Loving God,
On the day we presented our child for Baptism, he/she was welcomed into your family with great joy.
Help us to honour the promises we made to be his/her first and best teachers in the ways of faith.
May we give our children the best example we can as they try to live their lives in the way that Jesus taught us.
Amen.

Well done! You have come to the end of this part of the journey in preparing for your First Holy Communion. It doesn't finish here though! **This is only the beginning** of many more great days to come. After you celebrate your First Holy Communion, you can receive Communion every time you go to Mass.

Can you remember the six things that happen at Mass?

1. We gather together to _____.
2. We celebrate God's _____.
3. We listen to the _____ __ _____.
4. We give _____.
5. We share _____, the _____ __ _____.
6. We ___ in _____.

Each time you share in Holy Communion, **the Risen Jesus will be with you** in a special way. You can show that you are a friend of Jesus by showing that you love God and other people. That is what Jesus taught us.

PJ Prayer

Loving God,
Thank you for all the people who have helped me to prepare for my First Holy Communion, especially my family, my teacher and my priest.
Help me to keep learning about you and your love for the world.
Keep us all safe through the night.
Amen.

Prayers for the Mass

INTRODUCTORY RITES
Priest
In the name of the Father, and of the Son, and of the Holy Spirit.
People
Amen.

GREETINGS
Priest
The grace of our Lord Jesus Christ,
and the love of God,
and the communion of the Holy Spirit
be with you all.
Or
Grace to you and peace from God our Father
and the Lord Jesus Christ.
Or
The Lord be with you.
People
And with your spirit.

PENITENTIAL ACT A
I confess to almighty God
and to you, my brothers and sisters,
that I have greatly sinned,
in my thoughts and in my words,
in what I have done and in what I have failed to do,
through my fault, through my fault,
through my most grievous fault;
therefore I ask blessed Mary ever-Virgin,
all the Angels and Saints,
and you, my brothers and sisters,
to pray for me to the Lord our God.

PENITENTIAL ACT B
Priest
Have mercy on us, O Lord.
People
For we have sinned against you.
Priest
Show us, O Lord, your mercy.
People
And grant us your salvation.

KYRIE
Lord, have mercy.
Lord, have mercy.
Christ, have mercy.
Christ, have mercy.
Lord, have mercy.
Lord, have mercy.

GLORIA
Glory to God in the highest,
and on earth peace to people of good will.

We praise you,
we bless you,
we adore you,
we glorify you,
we give you thanks for your great glory,
Lord God, heavenly King,
O God, almighty Father.

Lord Jesus Christ, Only Begotten Son,
Lord God, Lamb of God, Son of the Father,
you take away the sins of the world,
have mercy on us;
you take away the sins of the world,
receive our prayer;
you are seated at the right hand of the Father,
have mercy on us.

For you alone are the Holy One,
you alone are the Lord,
you alone are the Most High,
Jesus Christ,
with the Holy Spirit,
in the glory of God the Father.
Amen.

LITURGY OF THE WORD

After the reading
Priest
The word of the Lord.
People
Thanks be to God.

Dialogue before the Gospel
Priest
The Lord be with you.
People
And with your spirit.

Dialogue after the Gospel
Priest
The Gospel of the Lord.
People
Praise to you Lord Jesus Christ.

Nicene Creed
I believe in one God,
the Father almighty,
maker of heaven and earth,
of all things visible and invisible.

I believe in one Lord Jesus
    Christ,
the Only Begotten Son of God,
born of the Father before all
    ages.
God from God, Light from
    Light,
true God from true God,
begotten, not made,
    consubstantial with the
    Father;

through him all things were
    made.
For us men and for our
    salvation
he came down from heaven,
and by the Holy Spirit was
    incarnate of the
Virgin Mary,
and became man.

For our sake he was crucified
    under Pontius Pilate,
he suffered death and was
    buried,
and rose again on the third day
in accordance with the
    Scriptures.
He ascended into heaven
and is seated at the right hand
    of the Father.

He will come again in glory
to judge the living and the
    dead
and his kingdom will have no
    end.

I believe in the Holy Spirit, the
    Lord, the giver of life,
who proceeds from the Father
    and the Son,
who with the Father and the
    Son is adored
and glorified,
who has spoken through the
    prophets.

I believe in one, holy, catholic
    and apostolic Church.
I confess one Baptism for the
    forgiveness of sins
and I look forward to the
    resurrection of the dead
and the life of the world to
    come. Amen.

Apostles' Creed
I believe in God,
the Father almighty,
Creator of heaven and earth,
and in Jesus Christ, his only
    Son, our Lord,
who was conceived by the Holy
    Spirit,
born of the Virgin Mary,
suffered under Pontius Pilate,
was crucified, died and was
    buried;
he descended into hell;
on the third day he rose again
    from the dead;
he ascended into heaven,
and is seated at the right hand
    of God the Father almighty;
from there he will come to
    judge the living and the dead.

I believe in the Holy Spirit,
the holy catholic Church,
the communion of saints,
the forgiveness of sins,
the resurrection of the body,
and life everlasting. Amen.

LITURGY OF THE EUCHARIST

Priest

Blessed are you, Lord God of all creation,

for through your goodness we have received the bread we offer you:

fruit of the earth and work of human hands,

it will become for us the bread of life.

People

Blessed be God for ever.

Priest

Blessed are you, Lord God of all creation,

for through your goodness we have received the wine we offer you:

fruit of the vine and work of human hands,

it will become our spiritual drink.

People

Blessed be God for ever.

Priest

Pray, brethren (brothers and sisters),

that my sacrifice and yours may be acceptable to God, the almighty Father.

People

May the Lord accept the sacrifice at your hands for the praise and glory of his name, for our good and the good of all his holy Church.

PREFACE DIALOGUE

Priest

The Lord be with you.

People

And with your spirit.

Priest

Lift up your hearts.

People

We lift them up to the Lord.

Priest

Let us give thanks to the Lord our God.

People

It is right and just.

SANCTUS

Holy, Holy, Holy Lord God of hosts.

Heaven and earth are full of your glory.

Hosanna in the highest.

Blessed is he who comes in the name of the Lord.

Hosanna in the highest.

MYSTERY OF FAITH (MEMORIAL ACCLAMATION)

Priest

The mystery of faith.

People

We proclaim your Death, O Lord,

and profess your Resurrection

until you come again.

Or

When we eat this Bread and drink this Cup,

we proclaim your Death, O Lord,

until you come again.

Or

Save us, Saviour of the world,

for by your Cross and Resurrection

you have set us free.

Or

My Lord and my God.

COMMUNION RITE

The Lord's Prayer

Priest

At the Saviour's command and formed by divine teaching,

we dare to say:

People

Our Father, who art in heaven,

hallowed be thy name;
thy kingdom come,
thy will be done
on earth as it is in heaven.
Give us this day our daily
bread,
and forgive us our
trespasses,
as we forgive those who
trespass against us;
and lead us not into
temptation,
but deliver us from evil.

Priest
Deliver us, Lord, we pray,
from every evil,
graciously grant peace in our
days,
that, by the help of your
mercy,
we may be always free from
sin
and safe from all distress,
as we await the blessed hope
and the coming of our
Saviour, Jesus Christ.

People
For the kingdom,
the power and the glory are
yours
now and for ever.

Sign of Peace
Priest
The peace of the Lord be
with you always.
People
And with your spirit.
Priest
Let us offer each other the
sign of peace.

Agnus Dei
Lamb of God, you take away
the sins of the world,
have mercy on us.
Lamb of God, you take away
the sins of the world,
have mercy on us.
Lamb of God, you take away
the sins of the world,
grant us peace.

INVITATION TO HOLY COMMUNION
Priest
Behold the Lamb of God,
behold him who takes away
the sins of the world.
Blessed are those called to
the supper of the Lamb.
People
Lord, I am not worthy
that you should enter under
my roof,
but only say the word
and my soul shall be healed.

WHEN RECEIVING COMMUNION
Priest
The Body of Christ.
People
Amen.

CONCLUDING RITES
Priest
The Lord be with you.
People
And with your spirit.
Priest
May almighty God bless you,
the Father, and the Son,
and the Holy Spirit.
People
Amen.

DISMISSAL
Priest
Go forth, the Mass is ended.
Or
Go and announce the Gospel
of the Lord.
Or
Go in peace, glorifying the
Lord by your life.
Or
Go in peace.
People
Thanks be to God.

Certificate of First Holy Communion

Awarded to

....
Write your name here

I celebrated my First Communion on

....
Write the date

Stick a photo of yourself in this box.

These people helped me to prepare:

....
My Family

....
My Teacher

....
My Priest